Intuition

Journal

With Inspirational Quotes

Trust your
Inner
Knowing

D1408855

Praise for
Inspirational Quotation Journals

I've journaled for years, but I love the idea of an Intuition Journal, just for all these "vibes" that I get about things. Yes, I am using this regularly.

Cathie Maloney, Boston, MA

Journaling is a painless way to find your direction in life. It clarifies the mind, accesses the heart and allows you go identify what is important to you.

Andrea Leblanc, Chicago, Ill

I often give journals as gifts, so I bought this for a friend. But by the time I'd read the introduction and a few of the quotes, I was already writing in it! So now I have to buy another for my friend and hope it arrives in time to give her for her birthday.

Marianne Simmons, Cardiff, Wales

The Intuition Inspirational Quotation Journal

From www.myinspirationaljournals.com

Keeping you inspired!

The more you trust your intuition, the more empowered you become, the stronger you become, and the happier you become.

Gisele Bundchen

Introduction to the Intuition Journal with Inspirational Quotes

Question: Why journal about Intuition?

Answer: Because by writing down what your intuition is telling you, you prevent your mind playing tricks on you.

You feel something and at the time you feel it, you write it down. So later, when you think "Did I really feel that?" or "Maybe it was really ..... I was feeling" you have the written proof of exactly what you felt and what you heard from your inner voice.

So in this way you can learn to trust more and more in that whispering voice within. It is never wrong. But sometimes we need some help getting used to believing it.

If you already trust your intuition implicitly it is also good to write it down, again, just so you remember it just the way it came, not changed, expanded or contracted by subsequent events.

Your intuition is a wonderful guide to your life. The more you can tune into it the more you can live your life in harmony with your inner self, which in turn creates less stress and tension, more happiness, more success.

When you read the quotes which come with every journaling page, some by people you will have heard of, some not, you will find encouragement to trust your "gut" even more. It is quite amazing how so many people attribute their success to intuition.

Intuition works. But sometimes we are afraid to trust it. After all we cannot feel, see or touch it. It does not come with a written guarantee that this is indeed intuition and not wishful thinking, or fear or any other emotion interfering and appearing to us as intuition.

When you write down what you think your inner voice is telling you, if there is any interference, if you are allowing other feelings to appear as intuition, you will find out as you re-read what you wrote later, once things have developed in that area of your life.

And this in turn will help you understand in the future what is indeed your inner being giving you guidance and what is not. You will learn to differentiate between them. For most people, that does not take long.

 Intuition is a natural part of being human so it is more a case of **un-**learning a learnt behavior (of not trusting it) rather than having to learn anything new. Hidden deep inside is still your natural inclination to believe in it. In our natural state, we would instinctively trust our intuition.

For most people, however, what they hear is indeed their intuition and what they need is the help to take more risks, put more credibility into what it tells them. Journaling regularly on what they hear, then journaling on the outcome later, is the key to solidifying that trust.

So every time you just feel you "know" something, or "feel" something, write it in this journal. If you feel it needs quite a bit of explanation as to what it "looks" like, then write that too. Or if it is very self-explanatory, perhaps just a short entry will do this time.

It is also good to write about how you are affected emotionally by what your intuition appears to be telling. Are you excited and happy?

Are you a bit scared? Is it something you've been trying to work out and all of a sudden the answer is clear to you?

Another gift of journaling is that the activity of thinking things through and writing them down activates your intuition if it is not already giving you a signal about a given situation.

So that is another way to use this journal.

If something is troubling you, or you have a decision to make etc., write about it in your journal. Talk to yourself on paper, or if you prefer, you can just talk it over with yourself verbally (silently or audibly), to clarify the situation in your mind and heart.

Just keep talking it through. It may bring tears, it may bring fear, it may bring excitement and joy. That obviously depends on the topic. But if you talk about it through and through, at some point you may suddenly just see the answer.

That is your intuition responding to the information and the time you have given to understanding it.

I will give you a brief example of something that happened to me just today.

I had an uncomfortable feeling that something I look like "having to do" (because the alternative is even less desirable) would not work out well, and I was feeling quite stressed that I was caught between two difficult situations.

I sat down and just wrote it all out for myself: what was worrying me, what I could see as being the various possible outcomes etc. I discussed it with myself for - it must have been - about half an hour.

Then suddenly I could just see the solution. It was as clear as day.

And at that point I lost all connection with the problem. I now just know how I will proceed and although I am still not certain of how it will work out, I know, I absolutely know, that this is the right course of action.

My intuition spoke to me when I gave it all the facts and feelings surrounding the issue.

Your intuition can do the same for you, and journaling can be a big part of making that happen, more often and more clearly.

I suggest that when you write down something that seems to be coming from your intuition and you don't yet know how it will show up in your life, mark it with a highlighter pen.

This way you know it is something to read again at various times until one day you will read it and realize your intuition was right on that point and you can write that in and use as proof for yourself when, at some point in the future, you are doubting.

There is also a handy index at the back of your Intuition Journal where you can jot down page number, or dates and a short note of what is written at that location.

This will make it easier to find where you wrote down your intuitive "message" and read how accurate it was when the answer or outcome appears.

We have an inner knowing to guide us through life. It is called Intuition. This journal is to capture its wisdom, to help you with your life and by creating that trust, will allow you to go with intuition more and more in the future.

So journal freely. Journal openly and journal often.

Happy Journaling.

Intuition Journal with Inspirational Quotes:
Trust your Inner Knowing

Start Journaling on the next page...

Listen to your intuition.
It will tell you everything you
need to know.

Anthony J. D'Angelo

Date:

Trusting our intuition often saves us from disaster.

Anne Wilson Schaef

Date:

How much trust did you give your intuition Today:
⬤⬤⬤⬤⬤ 5   ⬤⬤⬤⬤4   ⬤⬤⬤3   ⬤⬤2
or - Tomorrow will be better ⬤   Page 11

Intuition is a spiritual faculty and does not
explain, but simply points the way.

Florence Scovel Shinn

Date:

There is a universal, intelligent, life force that exists within everyone and everything. It resides within each one of use as a deep wisdom, an inner knowing. We can access this wonderful source of knowledge and wisdom through our intuition, an inner sense that tells us what feels right and true for us at any given moment.

Shakti Gawain

Date:

My intuition comes up with better stuff
than my head, I think.

Ben Whishaw

Date:

Most of my choices come about through some kind of intuition or instinct, and if I need to, I'll post-rationalize them, intellectually, afterwards. But generally, they come about just by feeling.

Joe Wright

Date:

How much trust did you give your intuition Today:

●●●●● 5 ●●●●●4 ●●●3 ●●2

or - Tomorrow will be better ●

Cease trying to work everything out with your minds. It will get you nowhere. Live by intuition and inspiration and let your whole life be Revelation.

Eileen Caddy

Date:

Listen to your instincts: if your gut says that there's something wrong - there is!

Unknown

Date:

Give yourself permission to immediately walk away from anything that gives you bad vibes. There is no need to explain or make sense of it. Just trust the little inner voice when it's telling you.

Unknown

Date:

_____

How much trust did you give your intuition Today:
⚫⚫⚫⚫⚫ 5   ⚫⚫⚫⚫ 4   ⚫⚫⚫ 3   ⚫⚫ 2
or - Tomorrow will be better ⚫   Page 25

A woman knows by intuition, or instinct, what is best for herself.

Marilyn Monroe

Date:

How much trust did you give your intuition Today:
5 4 3 2
or - Tomorrow will be better

Intuition comes very close to clairvoyance;
it appears to be the extrasensory
perception of reality.

Alexis Carrel

Date:

Intuition is the key to everything, in painting, filmmaking, business - everything. I think you could have an intellectual ability, but if you can sharpen your intuition, which they say is emotion and intellect joining together, then knowingness occurs.

David Lynch

How much trust did you give your intuition Today:
5   4   3   2
or - Tomorrow will be better

Page 31

Follow your intuition,
listening to your dreams,
your inner voice to guide you.

Katori Hall

Date:

You know what you need to know. You have your own personal built in GPS. Trust it – it always knows how to get you there and how to miss the worst of the traffic jams.

Unknown

Often you have to rely on intuition.

Bill Gates

How much trust did you give your intuition Today:

⬤⬤⬤⬤⬤ 5   ⬤⬤⬤⬤ 4   ⬤⬤⬤ 3   ⬤⬤ 2

or - Tomorrow will be better ⬤

The best thing you can do from this day forward is to follow your intuition. Take risks. Don't just make the safe and easy choices because you're afraid of what could happen. If you do, very little worth remembering will ever happen.

Unknown

Date:

How much trust did you give your intuition Today:

⬤⬤⬤⬤⬤ 5   ⬤⬤⬤⬤ 4   ⬤⬤⬤ 3   ⬤⬤ 2

or - Tomorrow will be better ⬤

A woman uses her intelligence to find reasons to support her intuition.

Gilbert K. Chesterton

Date:

A lady is smarter than a gentleman. Maybe she can sew a fine seam, she can have a baby, she can use her intuition instead of her brain, but she can't fold a paper in a crowded train.

Phyllis McGinley

Run away from laziness; work hard. Touch intuition and listen to the heart, not marketing directors. Dream.

Alber Elbaz

Date:

I was a litigation lawyer. That's all very logical. Become a litigation lawyer. Become successful. Have a nice office. But there was some pull inside of me saying, self-publish this book. I followed that intuition and it's been a great choice for me in my life.

Robin Sharma

Date:

How much trust did you give your intuition Today:

5   4   3   2

or - Tomorrow will be better

You must train your intuition - you must trust the small voice inside you which tells you exactly what to say, what to decide.

Ingrid Bergman

God gave women intuition and femininity.
Used properly, the combination easily
jumbles the brain of any man I've ever met.

Farrah Fawcett

No matter how deep a study you make. What you really have to rely on is your own intuition and when it comes down to it, you really don't know what's going to happen until you do it.

Konosuke Matsushita

How much trust did you give your intuition Today:

5   4   3   2

or - Tomorrow will be better

I have an intuition, and usually my intuition is right. I have a feeling for whether a role will be good or bad for me, and I almost never make a mistake.

Anna Netrebko

Intuition is seeing with the soul.

Dean Koontz

Date:

How much trust did you give your intuition Today:
⬤⬤⬤⬤⬤ 5   ⬤⬤⬤⬤ 4   ⬤⬤⬤ 3   ⬤⬤ 2
or - Tomorrow will be better ⬤

If you trust in everything the world tells you, you can't develop your own intuition about what's right or wrong. Start believing in your own intuitions they are the green light towards your life.

Unknown

Date:

How much trust did you give your intuition Today:

⬤⬤⬤⬤⬤ 5   ⬤⬤⬤⬤ 4   ⬤⬤⬤ 3   ⬤⬤ 2

or - Tomorrow will be better ⬤

You have to leave the city of your comfort and go into the wilderness of your intuition. What you'll discover will be wonderful. What you'll discover is yourself.

Alan Alda

Date:

How much trust did you give your intuition Today:

5   4   3   2

or - Tomorrow will be better

Everything I do is just really my intuition, and every time I go against my intuition, it's a mistake. Even though I may sit down and analyze and intellectualize something on paper, if I go against my gut feeling, it's wrong.

Tamara Mellon

Date:

How much trust did you give your intuition Today:

5 4 3 2

or - Tomorrow will be better

Don't try to comprehend with your mind. Your minds are very limited. Use your intuition.

Madeleine L'Engle

Date:

_____

_____

_____

_____

_____

_____

_____

_____

_____

_____

_____

_____

_____

_____

_____

_____

_____

How much trust did you give your intuition Today:

●●●●● 5   ●●●●● 4   ●●●● 3   ●● 2

or - Tomorrow will be better ●

I believe in intuitions and inspirations...I sometimes feel that I am right. I do not know that I am.

Albert Einstein

Date:

How much trust did you give your intuition Today:

⬤⬤⬤⬤⬤ 5   ⬤⬤⬤⬤ 4   ⬤⬤⬤ 3   ⬤⬤ 2

or - Tomorrow will be better ⬤

Listen to your instincts: if your gut says that there's something wrong - there is!

Unknown

I feel there are two people inside me - me and my intuition. If I go against her, she'll screw me every time, and if I follow her, we get along quite nicely.

Kim Basinger

Date:

Some people say there's nothing new under the sun. I still think that there's room to create.
And intuition doesn't necessarily come from under this sun.
It comes from within.

Pharrell Williams

How much trust did you give your intuition Today:

●●●●● 5   ●●●●4   ●●●3   ●●2

or - Tomorrow will be better ●

Insight is not a light bulb that goes off inside our heads. It is a flickering candle that can easily be snuffed out.

Malcolm Gladwell

Date:

How much trust did you give your intuition Today:

●●●●● 5   ●●●●● 4   ●●●● 3   ●● 2

or - Tomorrow will be better ●

Follow your heart, never surrender your dreams. Always believe in yourself and let God do the rest.

Unknown

Date:

How much trust did you give your intuition Today:
●●●●● 5   ●●●●4   ●●●3   ●●2
or - Tomorrow will be better ●

Cease trying to work everything out with your minds. It will get you nowhere. Live by intuition and inspiration and let your whole life be Revelation.

Eileen Caddy

It is always with excitement that I wake up in the morning wondering what my intuition will toss up to me, like gifts from the sea. I work with it and rely on it.
It's my partner.

Jonas Salk

Intuition is the supra-logic that cuts out all the routine processes of thought and leaps straight from the problem to the answer.

Robert Graves

Date:

It is through science that we prove, but through intuition that we discover.

Henri Poincare

Nobody taught Picasso how to paint - he learned for himself. And nobody can teach you to be a producer. You can learn the mechanics, but you can't learn what's right about a script or a director or an actor. That comes from instinct and intuition. It comes from inside you.

Dino De Laurentiis

◯ Date:

How much trust did you give your intuition Today:
●●●●● 5   ●●●●4   ●●●3   ●●2
or - Tomorrow will be better ●   Page 87

Life is about learning from the past, trusting your intuition going forward, taking chances, finding moments of happiness, and realizing everything is simply a lesson that happens for a reason.

Unknown

Date:

Intuition will tell the thinking mind where to look next.

Jonas Salk

Date:

You must trust your instinct, intuition and judgment.

Rouben Mamoulian

Date:

The concept of psychic energy is easy for most people to imagine. After all, it's just one step beyond intuition - and almost everyone is comfortable with the idea of intuition.

Jayne Ann Krentz

Date:

All great men are gifted with intuition.
They know without reasoning or analysis,
what they need to know.

Alexis Carrel

Date:

How much trust did you give your intuition Today:
●●●●● 5　●●●●4　●●●3　●●2
or - Tomorrow will be better ●　　　　　Page 97

The truth about life and lies about life are not measured by others but by your intuition, which never lies.

Santosh Kalwar

Intuition becomes increasingly valuable in the new information society precisely because there is so much data.

John Naisbitt

Date:

My gut and intuition told me it wasn't time to do this.

Mario Vazquez

Date:

How much trust did you give your intuition Today:
5 4 3 2
or - Tomorrow will be better   Page 103

Sometimes you have got to be able to listen
to yourself and be okay with no one else
understanding.

Unknown

Date:

How much trust did you give your intuition Today:
●●●●● 5   ●●●●4   ●●●3   ●●2
or - Tomorrow will be better ●   Page 105

Your intuition will tell you where you need to go; it will connect you with people you should meet; it will guide you toward work that is meaningful for you - work that brings you joy, work that feels right for you.

Shakti Gawain

Date:

How much trust did you give your intuition Today:
5   4   3   2
or - Tomorrow will be better

I guess if you have an original take on life, or something about you is original, you don't have to study people who came before you. You don't have to mimic anybody. You just have a gut feeling inside, an instinct that tells you what's right for you, and you can't do it in any other way.

Barbra Streisand

I always trust my gut reaction;

it's always right.

Kiana Tom

Date:

I've only ever trusted my gut on everything.
I don't trust my head, I don't trust my
heart, I trust my gut.

Bryan Adams

Date:

Anytime I listen to my gut and I don't do something, or I do, it always tends to work out in my favor.

Mandy Moore

It's been very important for me to follow
my gut or my heart, or whichever organ you
want
to go by.

Lili Taylor

Date:

How much trust did you give your intuition Today:
⚘⚘⚘⚘⚘ 5   ⚘⚘⚘⚘ 4   ⚘⚘⚘ 3   ⚘⚘ 2
or - Tomorrow will be better ⚘

Make sure that you always follow your heart and your gut, and let yourself be who you want to be, and who you know you are. And don't let anyone steal your joy.

Jonathan Groff

Date:

Sometimes all you have is instinct, a gut feeling. It's important to pay attention to them.

Unknown

Date:

How much trust did you give your intuition Today:
5   4   3   2
or - Tomorrow will be better

You know the truth by the way it feels.

Unknown

Date:

To succeed, you need to take that gut feeling in what you believe and act on it with all of your heart.

Christy Borgeld

Date:

How much trust did you give your intuition Today:
5   4   3   2
or - Tomorrow will be better   Page 125

I loved my life, but my choices were overloading and overwhelming me. Listening to inner feelings and fulfilling some of these urges when they come along is incredibly important.

Pamela Stephenson

☀ Date:

How much trust did you give your intuition Today:
⚙⚙⚙⚙⚙ 5   ⚙⚙⚙⚙ 4   ⚙⚙⚙ 3   ⚙⚙ 2
or - Tomorrow will be better ⚙   Page 127

Your mind knows only some things. Your inner voice, your instinct, knows everything. If you listen to what you know instinctively, it will always lead you down the right path.

Henry Winkler

Date:

When I'm hiring someone I look for magic and a spark. Little things that intuitively give me a gut feeling that this person will go to the ends of the earth to accomplish the task at hand.

Tommy Mottola

How much trust did you give your intuition Today:

5   4   3   2

or - Tomorrow will be better

It's good to say, 'Look, I can't always be right, but my gut tells me this' - and then you confirm with your gut.

Robert Redford

Date:

How much trust did you give your intuition Today:

5   4   3   2

or - Tomorrow will be better

I don't make decisions with my head anymore. If I don't get the go ahead with my gut, I usually back out.

Jane Siberry

Date:

How much trust did you give your intuition Today:
5   4   3   2
or - Tomorrow will be better

Have the courage to follow your heart and intuition. They somehow already know what you truly want to become.

Steve Jobs

Date:

How much trust did you give your intuition Today:
5 4 3 2
or - Tomorrow will be better
Page 137

Find the passion, that gut feeling you have.
Find it, stick to it and see what happens.

Alexandra Stratta

Date:

How much trust did you give your intuition Today:

5   4   3   2

or - Tomorrow will be better

I think one great tip is that you should always love yourself. If you don't love yourself, take care of yourself, cater to yourself and that little inner voice, you will really not be very worthy of being with someone else, because you won't be the best version of you.

Kimora Lee Simmons

Date:

How much trust did you give your intuition Today:
5   4   3   2
or - Tomorrow will be better   Page 141

Keep the faith, don't lose your perseverance and always trust your gut instinct.

Paula Abdul

I design from instinct. It's the only way I know how to live. What feels good. What feels right. What is needed. Give me a problem and I will approach it creatively, from my gut.

Donna Karan

Date:

How much trust did you give your intuition Today:
⚫⚫⚫⚫⚫ 5   ⚫⚫⚫⚫4   ⚫⚫⚫3   ⚫⚫2
or - Tomorrow will be better ⚫   Page 145

Trust your hunches... hunches are usually based on facts files away just below the conscious level.

Dr. Joyce Brothers

Date:

Trust your instinct to the end – even
though you can render no reason.

Unknown

Intuition is the highest form of intelligence, transcending all individual abilities and skills.

Sylvia Clare

You have to master not only the art of listening to your head, you must also master listening to your heart and listening to your gut.

Carly Fiorina

⚙ Date:

How much trust did you give your intuition Today:
⚙⚙⚙⚙⚙ 5   ⚙⚙⚙⚙ 4   ⚙⚙⚙ 3   ⚙⚙ 2
or - Tomorrow will be better ⚙   Page 153

Again, you can't connect the dots looking forward; you can only connect them looking backwards. So you have to trust that the dots will somehow connect in your future. You have to trust in something - your gut, destiny, life, karma, whatever. This approach has never let me down, and it has made all the difference in my life.

Steve Jobs

● Date:

Handy Memory Jogger Index

Handy Memory Jogger Index

Date/Page   Quote ☐   Journal Entry ☐
Notes:

Date/Page   Quote ☐   Journal Entry ☐
Notes:

Date/Page   Quote ☐   Journal Entry ☐
Notes:

Date/Page   Quote ☐   Journal Entry ☐
Notes:

Date/Page   Quote ☐   Journal Entry ☐
Notes:

Date/Page   Quote ☐   Journal Entry ☐
Notes:

Date/Page   Quote ☐   Journal Entry ☐
Notes:

Date/Page   Quote ☐   Journal Entry ☐
Notes:

Date/Page   Quote ☐   Journal Entry ☐
Notes:

Date/Page   Quote ☐   Journal Entry ☐
Notes:

Date/Page   Quote ☐   Journal Entry ☐
Notes:

Date/Page   Quote ☐   Journal Entry ☐
Notes:

Date/Page   Quote ☐   Journal Entry ☐
Notes:

Date/Page   Quote ☐   Journal Entry ☐
Notes:

Date/Page   Quote ☐   Journal Entry ☐
Notes:

Date/Page   Quote ☐   Journal Entry ☐
Notes:

Date/Page   Quote ☐   Journal Entry ☐
Notes:

Date/Page   Quote ☐   Journal Entry ☐
Notes:

Date/Page   Quote ☐   Journal Entry ☐
Notes:

Date/Page   Quote ☐   Journal Entry ☐
Notes:

Date/Page   Quote ☐   Journal Entry ☐
Notes:

Date/Page   Quote ☐   Journal Entry ☐
Notes:

Date/Page   Quote ☐   Journal Entry ☐
Notes:

Date/Page   Quote ☐   Journal Entry ☐
Notes:

Date/Page   Quote ☐   Journal Entry ☐
Notes:

Date/Page   Quote ☐   Journal Entry ☐
Notes:

Date/Page   Quote ☐   Journal Entry ☐
Notes:

Date/Page   Quote ☐   Journal Entry ☐
Notes:

About the Author:

Fiona MacKay Young is a Personal Development & Career Coach who uses the tool of journaling both with clients and for herself.

She has journaled for most of her life, and found it extremely helpful as a tool for motivation, creativity and generally keeping her life on an even keel.

Fiona has developed her Inspirational Quotation Journals to help others maximize on the benefits of writing from the heart on a regular basis. She totally believes that this is a tool to improve life, better relationships and generally enjoy all that life has to offer.

Fiona spends her time between the Pacific West Coast and various parts of the British Isles.

You can contact Fiona at fionamackayyoung@gmail.com.

Made in the USA
Lexington, KY
05 July 2018